TOCABAGA 2
THEOTERRORISM

THOMAS H. WARD

TOCABAGA 2:

Theoterrorism

THE TOCABAGA CHRONICLES

by

THOMAS H. WARD

ISBN-13: 978-0615910307

ISBN-10: 0615910300

Transcendent Publishing
121 104th Ave. Treasure Island, FL 33706
www.transcendentpublishing.com

If you are reading this then you are one of the lucky ones or smart ones who have survived the first year of the collapse. I am writing these chronicles to pass on a history of what has happened, a history telling how we have survived so far. I do not reveal the full names of the people living here in case the Feds happen to read these chronicles. Read my story and tell others what has happened here. Pass it on; it may save your life.

My name is Jack Gunn and I live on Tocabaga. The real name will not be given, nor the location. Tocabaga is a clue as to the general location of this island. It is a sanctuary where one can be safe from what is going on in the outside world. If you happen to come here, are of good character, and believe in the freedom of man and the Constitution, you are welcome to stay. The current population is 556 people. We help each other stay alive.

We are waiting for you to contact us by email to find out where Tocabaga is located. There is an email address hidden within these chronicles. Tocabaga is a real location.

I will reply,
Jack Gunn

MAY 9, 2025
Last entry – April 25, 2025

We held a vote for President of our compound and Rick won, not many wanted that job. Everyone likes Rick and he has a certain way of making you listen to him. Maybe it is his deep voice or his reasonable logic. Rick has a brother who is an FBI agent that he hasn't seen for years. Rick is a self-made millionaire who owned a tow truck company. He has no military experience to speak of.

Years ago when Rick and I use to go shooting many people would ask us what is the best type of gun to buy? Buying a gun can be confusing since there are so many types of guns and different calibers. So I wrote an article named "GUN SELECTION" which was published on the internet. I have included this article at the end of these chronicles to help you select the proper weapon. Read this article and pass on the information to your friends.

I was elected Vice President and Director of Security because no one else wanted the job, maybe because I had the most experience having actually killed more people than anyone else, other than my son.

I have had many different jobs in my life. I spent four years in the Army as a Military Policeman, and was trained how to use handguns, rifles, shotguns, and hand-to-hand combat. I once worked for a government Contractor in Security and had a DOD (Department of Defense) secret clearance and AEC (Atomic Energy Commission) security clearance.

I often ponder, how did our country get this way? My thinking is it was a number of things but it was also an overzealous President who was pushing for more control of the government to make a truly socialist state.

The President started a draft, but not for the military, for the new Federal Police Force or FPF. Their job would be to start green safe zones in the cities and guard the electric power plants and water supplies. They were to keep things running normal and generally enforce the laws. The Federal Police have all the same weapons, trucks, and tanks that the Army does. There are now 50,000 new Policemen. Even this number cannot control the situation.

The President put into effect Presidential Executive Order 13603 which to everyone's surprise declares that all property belongs to the Federal Government: your house, money, guns, and even your kids. They can tell you where to live and where to work.

Years before, things were not making much sense especially when the government took control of the news media. It became state owned so the only news we received was what the Federal Government wanted us to see. Back in 2013, the NSA started to tap our phones, read our emails, read our snail mail, and read our Facebook pages. We were all being watched, we were all suspected of doing something wrong, we were all having our Bill of Rights violated in the name of government security, and no one did anything about it.

Benjamin Franklin once said, "He who sacrifices freedom for security deserves neither."

Unemployment shot up to 55% and everyone knew that things were changing as more and more acts of violence were reported across the nation. Riots, robberies, shootings, explosions, and even attacks on police stations were common. Some states called up the National Guard to help maintain control as desperate people do desperate things. Just driving to the grocery store was becoming dangerous. You needed to carry a gun for safety or your trip to the store could end up being your last.

Our currency became worthless due to inflation and the government closed all the banks to stop bank runs. A loaf of bread is $100 and milk is $150 per gallon, if you can find it. People have run out of money and even if they have any in the bank, they cannot get it. Savings accounts are wiped out and if you have any gold or silver in the bank forget it, the doors are locked. The government is taking it all because the country is bankrupt.

For many years illegal aliens have been coming across the border from Mexico. But not all the people are hardworking Mexicans looking for work. The fact is many of those crossing the border are from the Middle East and are related to Islamic radical terrorist groups. How do I know this, because the US Government has admitted that every year several thousand manage to sneak into the USA.

In addition, the gangs and cartels that smuggle

dope are also making inroads into the US selling their crap to whatever idiots will buy it. These gangs have turf wars and during their wars they do not care whom they rob or kill. Then there is the drug user who robs and kills to get money to pay for their habit. Finally we have the radical groups like the Skinheads, Neo-Nazis, some extreme gangs, and those that want white supremacy.

The government is now controlling the food and there are food lines at every store. You must wait for hours to get any food. If you can buy any food it is only enough for a few days. You cannot feed your family on a loaf of bread. Fresh vegetables and fruit cannot be found. Everything is canned goods or freeze dried ready to eat meals. The question is can we change what we have become? There is no country to help us as they all have failed. We are the last hope of free mankind. We cannot forget the Bill of Rights, the US Constitution, and the fact we are One Nation under God.

MAY 10, 2025

Robbie my best friend was killed by the Feds on April 27, 2025 and was buried at sea like everyone else. We make white crosses out of plastic fence posts and paint the names of those that died and the dates they lived so they will be remembered. We included the six Rangers who were killed fighting for our freedom in our cross cemetery which is ringed by a small white picket fence. The Army took the Rangers' bodies away for burial at a National Cemetery. We had a 21-gun salute and ceremony for everyone who was killed fighting the FPF, the so-called Federal Police Force. Robbie was a Board member on Tocabaga and we voted to replace him with Jim Bo who is my son-in-law.

Everyone gets buried at sea here because we have no room for a cemetery and don't want dead bodies buried near us. The coyotes would dig them up and eat them. Coyotes are a dangerous problem after coming here in the year 2000. They are fast, smart and eat anything, even people, but they usually try to make easy kills of rabbits, cats, and dogs. We try to shoot them on sight but they are very elusive and roam mainly at night. One ran down the middle of the street in broad daylight the other day. It went by so fast most people did not see it.

One of the Rangers killed in the battle with the FPF had his wife and daughter coming here to live this month. We will greet her and make sure she is taken care of. Captain Sessions had the terrible job to make sure the dead Rangers' family members were contacted.

Captain Sessions is a 6 foot 180 pound man of good looks, has light brown hair and an ugly scar running across his cheek from a bullet wound. He has a very commanding air about him and his troops follow every order he gives them without question. There are a lot of tough men in the Rangers and Captain Sessions is one of the toughest I have seen. He is a smart battle hardened Ranger who cares about his men and they care about him. I like him because you can tell he is a man of his word.

The Rangers took all 65 FPF (Federal Police Force) prisoners that were captured during our battle on April 25, 2025, away by truck to a secure location, but they would not tell us where they were taken because of security reasons. Who knows, maybe they were all eliminated or terminated by the Rangers, as there were a lot of hard feelings. You could tell the Rangers hated the FPF and rightfully so in my opinion. Everyone hates the Feds and I am sure no one minds killing a few of them. I believe they should all face a firing squad and be shot for treason.

Since April 25th, we haven't had to do security duty since the Rangers handle everything in regards to our security and protection. They come to the bar for some of Eddie's beer when they get time off. We are all bonding very well and becoming good friends.

Our people spend most of the time trying to grow enough food and catch 1,000 pounds of fish per day. We have a lot of mouths to feed and 40 people go fishing almost every day. Many take out boats and go far offshore but most fish on the shoreline.

On April 27th, the rest of the Rangers arrived by truck, Hummers, and helicopters making a total of almost 600 men now based at the Fort. Everyone is happy about that as now we have real protection and a real sense of security. They are always flying in and out of the Fort on dangerous missions to fight crime or terrorism wherever it may be found. Usually about 200 men remain here at all times.

Captain Sessions gave us the ID badges to hand out to all our people. They hang around our necks on a silver chain and must be shown when we go into the Fort. Not many people want to leave the compound because it is still not safe on the mainland.

As promised by General Harper, Tony now has an ice machine and we have a huge generator, the size of a 60-foot truck to provide power for our freezers, and air conditioning in the Bank, three restaurants, church, and bar. The church has good attendance every Sunday by Rangers and other Christians.

We have no Muslims living here now but a friend of mine who is a Muslim contacted me the other day by cell phone. He believes in freedom and the Bill of Rights and wants to come here to live. His name is Aamir meaning civilized in Arabic; it certainly fits him.

7

At about 1600 hours, my radio hissed, "Jack, a guy named Aamir is at the Bridge and wants to see you."

I replied to Steve, "Tell him I will be right there. Oh, by the way he is a good guy so no need to worry about him."

Steve said, "He is with four other men."

"Ok, keep your eye on them. I don't know who they are."

My wife Hemmi heard the radio chatter and said, "Aamir. I wonder how his wife and daughter are doing."

"I will find out and let you know. Aamir probably wants come here to live."

"See you later, Honey. Make me a surprise for dinner tonight."

"Ok, but all we have is fish and rice."

"Great then make some grilled fish surprise with rice. That sounds good to me."

My son Tommy and I left my house after putting my Glock 17 in my holster and grabbing my AR 15 9mm carbine. The squeaky back door slammed shut on the way out. Jumping into my old 1997 Ford 4x4, which still runs great but the radio and odometer don't work, I drove to the bridge.

Years ago, Aamir used to come to the local bar for a beer where I met him. We became friends, and many times we discussed religion and terrorism. Aamir is from Morocco; he moved here and became a citizen to have a better life. He told me he hates al-Qaida and other extreme terrorist groups, as they want to run your life and tell you how to act and behave. My guess is he wants to come to Tocabaga to live. Aamir is five foot six 120 pounds, with jet-black hair, and dark eyes with a kind face.

"Tommy, I want you to meet a guy named Aamir and tell me what you think of him. He is a friend from a long time ago and he is a Muslim."

Tommy said, "A Muslim and you like him?"

"Yeah, he has always been nice to me and he thinks the way we do. He even drinks beer. I know a number of Muslims and they are just like us, only the radical's cause problems."

"Yep, that is true."

Arriving at the bridge we jumped out and ran up the small hill that the bridge forms and at the apex I saw Aamir holding a small white flag; he was under guard by the Rangers. Looking down the bridge where Iron Maiden was located there were four other men standing next to a car. I looked carefully at them but did not recognize any of them. None of them had weapons showing.

The Bradley named Gun Smoke had its machine guns at the ready and four Rangers were standing nearby watching them closely.

I reached out my hand to Aamir and said, "Hello, my friend, long time no see."

Aamir, a happy smiling guy, put out his hand to shake mine and replied with his Arabic accent, "Jack, it is great to see you. How is your family?"

"Great, Aamir, I would like you to meet my son Tommy. How is your family?"

"Tommy, it is my great pleasure to meet you. Your father use to talk about you all the time when you were in the Marines."

"Hello, Aamir, it is nice to meet you also."

"My wife and daughter are okay, but we could be better. I need your help Jack."

"How can I be of help to you?"

"Jack, there are 23 of us who need protection, food, and a safe place to live for our children. This island is the best place and we should have come here sooner, like you advised me a couple of years ago. Is that still possible? Why is the Army here?"

I was thinking, for a group of 23 to come here

would create problems, especially if radical violent groups such as al-Qaida ever attacked us. The question is which side Aamir and his people would choose to fight with. This was very risky because they would be walking around here with weapons. I don't know if I can really trust Aamir and since I do not know all of his people it is a very unsure situation. I have known Aamir on and off for about 15 years, sometimes Aamir could be a hot head and lose his temper quickly. I often wondered if Aamir had any ties to extremist because of all the trips he would take overseas each year for 2 or 3 weeks at a time. Trips like that cost a lot of money and he did not make that kind of money years ago working as a waiter.

Many of our people do not care for Muslims since 9-11. All these years we have been fighting al-Qaida all over the world and now they are here in the US cutting off heads and killing those that do not believe as they do. Rumor has it that there is a large group of 1000 men roaming around the country killing at will. There are also small groups of 5 to 10 men who seem to be good guys in the daytime but at night they become al-Qaida members. They are around so you need to be careful of strangers, as you never know whom you are talking too; you could get killed on the spot. The other problem is IED's or roadside bombs, which are being planted all over the place.

"Aamir, this island is now called Camp Tocabaga and Fort Desoto is an Army Ranger base. That is why you see the tanks and Rangers here guarding the bridge. To let your group come here would require a background check on all your people including you. I need to get the Army to approve first, and then our people would need to vote on letting your group in or not. I don't know all your people and letting them carry guns in our compound could present problem. So it is not an easy situation. If it was just you, your wife, and kid it would be a lot easier."

"What do you mean a background check?"

"Every adult would need to provide a DNA sample, have a picture taken along with finger prints and then Army Intelligence would check everyone to see if they are on any terrorist list, criminal list, or whatever."

"Jack that is bull shit we are all US citizens. It is discrimination on your part."

"No, not on my part, it is what the Army requires for security. Security comes first here, as there are over 1,000 people here. It's no different than going through security at the airport."

"I am wasting my time talking to you, get me the Army Big Shot to speak too right away! You cannot show discrimination just because we are Muslim!"

"Fine I will radio him to come and meet you but I suggest you simmer down first. Being a hot head, yelling at me will not help you one bit. I have known you a long time and I can tell you I don't care if you are Muslim. The Army doesn't care if you are Muslim but we do care if anyone is a potential terrorist."

I took out my radio, "Colonel Turner, this is Jack Gunn at the bridge. Can you come here to meet some people who want to live in our compound? Over."

The radio hissed back, "Jack, I will be there in about 30 minutes with Captain Sessions, over."

Waiting for Colonel Turner I asked Aamir, "Who are the other people in your group, how do you know them?"

"Five are my relatives and the others are from the local area. Most of them are my long time friends and I feel they can be trusted."

"Aamir, if any of these people fail a background check then everyone in your group is suspected as a potential problem. It gives you black eye so to speak."

"Jack, all I can say is bullshit to that thinking! I am really concerned about my kid and wife. We have six little kids under age ten. Can you just let the women and kids come here to live?"

"It is not up to me, Aamir. If it were I would agree to that."

Colonel Turner and Captain Sessions pulled up in their Hummer along with two Ranger guards. They jumped out of the Hummer and I said, "Colonel Turner, Sir, this is Aamir. Aamir this is Colonel Turner and Captain Sessions. The Colonel is in command here."

While shaking hands Turner said, "It is a pleasure to meet you, Sir."

Aamir replied, "The pleasure is mine, Jack told me that it is up to you to let people in to live here. Is that correct?"

"Yes that is correct, Aamir. Anyone coming here to live has to have a background check. This takes about one month."

"One month. That is no good we need to come here now. I told Jack this is discrimination because we are Muslim."

"Sir, I had no idea you were Muslim but it makes no difference to us if you are Muslim, Jewish or whatever your religion happens to be."

"Colonel Turner, what if just our wives and kids come here and not the men. Can you let them in sooner than one month?"

I butted in, "Aamir, why now after almost 2 years are you in such a hurry to protect your family? What is going on and why are you so worried? Aamir tell us the truth if you want us to help."

"Well the truth is they are coming and some are already here."

Captain Sessions replied, "Who is coming? Who is already here?"

"The al-Qaida Army. That is who and that is why I want my group here for protection."

Colonel Turner, Sessions, and I just looked at each other and no one said a word.

Everyone knows about al-Qaida; they are a Theoterrorism group. According to Oxford Dictionary, Theoterrorism is terrorism that has a religious motive or purpose.

I commented, "Look it is hot, let's get in the shade, have a cool drink, and talk more about this. I suggest we go down to the bar."

Aamir said, "Okay, just a minute, I need to tell my men I will be back soon."

Aamir yelled something to them in Arabic and they waved back to him.

Aamir, Tommy, and I drove to the bar in my truck and the Colonel and Captain followed behind us. On the way there, no one spoke a word.

Getting out of the truck, Aamir said, "Not much has changed here except the jungle is taking over the island."

Tommy replied, "Yeah that is one of our big problems, everything grows so fast here. We got a million rattle snakes here so watch where you walk."

We all laughed because we all hate snakes.

As we walked into the bar, Tony who knows Aamir said, "Aamir, how the hell are you doing?"

"Hey Tony, nice to see you again. You look the same as two years ago."

"Colonel, Sir, what do you guys want to drink?"

"Ice-cold cokes all around, Tony."

Tony gave us all an ice-cold coke with real ice. Everyone was a little more relaxed and not feeling the pressure of the hot steaming sun. An ice-cold coke always tastes damn good when you are hot and thirsty.

When I used to travel all around the world, there were two words that no matter where you went everyone knew. Those two words were OK and COKE.

Captain Sessions asked Aamir, "How do you know al-Qaida is coming here and how many men do they have?"

Aamir replied, "I am Arabic so I know; please do not ask how I know. I know a lot of information about al-Qaida that you do not. I can tell you the number of men is anywhere from 1,000 to 2,000. I know that they will kill anyone who is not of the same belief; they rape women, and take children as slaves. I do not want that to happen to my family."

Sessions asked, "Where is al-Qaida located?"

"I do not know exactly, they are everywhere in small groups of 5 to 10 men hiding out until it is time. Gentlemen, I beg you to let the women and children in. I must go now before it gets dark, we need to be at home when night time comes, but I will return tomorrow for your answer."

Tommy asked, "Aamir, you said hiding out until it is time. Time for what?"

"Time to attack here. I must leave here now before it gets dark; please take me back to the bridge. I will be back tomorrow at noon for your positive answer."

Aamir shook hands with the Colonel and Captain, and we drove him back to the bridge. It was tense and no one spoke on the way back.

Pulling up to the bridge I told Aamir, "I will do my best to convince the Colonel to let your kids and women come here. I suggest tomorrow if you know more information about what al-Qaida is planning and when then please share it, as that will be a big help to show you are with us. As for the men in your group, we will figure out something, somehow we will help you. I will do my best."

We shook hands and Aamir said, "Thank you, Jack and Tommy, peace be with you."

"Aamir, how is Rahim doing? Tell him I said

Hello."

"Rahim is doing fine. I will tell him hello from you."

Rahim is a mutual friend of ours. He is also a Muslim and a great guy. He looks like a big bear at six foot four and around 280 pounds. He is friendly and just wants to live in peace. He moved here from Morocco years ago and is a US citizen. I actually trust Rahim more than Aamir. I wonder why Rahim did not come here with Aamir since they are close friends.

"Thanks, Aamir, peace be with you also."

I walked with Aamir down to his car to get a better look at the other four men who were waiting for him. They looked at me and I looked at them. I bowed my head slightly and raised my hand as if to say hello. All did the same, except for one man who wore a black ball hat and black shirt. He did not move but just stared at me. I could tell looking into his eyes he did not like me. I could see the hate emanating from those black eyes; I had seen this hate before so I knew this guy was trouble. He was giving me the evil eye.

Aamir and his men jumped into the old car and slowly drove away as I watched.

Returning to the top of the bridge Tommy asked me, "Dad, where is he living at?"

"I don't know. Maybe I should have asked, but he didn't reveal that. I wonder why. Well Tommy, what did you think of Aamir?"

"To be honest I didn't care for his cocky attitude and the way he talked to you. If he were not your so-called friend, I would have beaten the shit out of him for yelling at you. I don't trust him. He seems very tricky. You asked me, so there you are. That's what I think."

Tommy is 5 foot 10 inches of solid muscle and is a hard core trained Marine and knows every trick in the book for hand to hand combat. Yes he could have beaten the shit out of Aamir but it would serve no purpose. Since he was a Marine Scout Sniper he also is an excellent shot and knows his weapons. He is a good looking young man with blond hair and bright blue eyes.

"Okay, thanks for the input and I agree with you. Aamir is not easy to understand and he always has had a chip on his shoulder. I don't fully trust him either and certainly not with my life. Did you see the guy in the black hat and shirt?"

"Yeah, what about him?"

"Well he gave me the evil eye, like he wanted to kill me. I have seen that look before and I know you have too."

"Yup, he just gave himself away. I think he will be a problem."

My radio came on, "Jack, this is Sessions, the Colonel and I are going back to the Fort and will contact the General to make some kind of plan. Let's meet at 0800 hours at the bar to discuss this before Aamir arrives at noon. Make sure Rick and anyone else you like are at the meeting."

"Okay, Captain, see you in the morning."

I was wondering how Aamir knew anything about al-Qaida. I wondered why he was keeping some secret. Where is the al-Qaida Army located and how many of them are there? It disturbed me that he was not more open with us since he wanted help so bad.

One thing for sure, we will be fighting al-Qaida in the near future but the big question is when. I wondered who the guy was that gave me the evil eye in the black hat. We will find out tomorrow one way or another. I will ask Aamir.

MAY 11, 2025

Last night I radioed Rick, and the other Board members to meet at 8am at the bar with Colonel Turner and Captain Sessions to discuss the situation.

Arriving at the bar, everyone was all ready there, along with Sergeant Cain. Sergeant Cain is the person in charge of the drones. I couldn't help but wonder what he was doing here.

Colonel Turner started out, "Gentlemen, I spoke to General Harper last night about the Muslim group coming here. He suggested that we take in the women and children for their safety. He also said no men can come in without a background check and that is final."

"His idea is to let the men be the . . . FRONT LINE . . . of defense and fight against al-Qaida with us. We will set up sand bag defensive positions on both sides of the road. We'll put up some tents for them up to live in temporarily and supply them food that their wives can take to them three times a day. After a background check they can come into Tocabaga assuming your group approves."

"Sergeant Cain has a report to give and pictures to show you taken by our drones. We have been watching groups of 5 to 10 men with weapons infiltrate the area around us for about a month."

"Thank you, Colonel Turner, Sir. Yes our drones have spotted these men coming to our area almost every day, for about a month. Our drones cover

21

an area of 30 miles and as you know can take very detailed pictures. There may be as many as 200 men down the road from here, about a mile in the old condos. Others are less than 5 miles away spread out in many buildings around the area. We believe these guys are al-Qaida.

"They have many different types of weapons including RPGs which is their weapon of choice. We have also seen them plant roadside bombs at night, which is an al-Qaida trick. The main thing to our advantage is they have no armored vehicles or aircraft. They get around by pickup trucks that have machine guns mounted in the back. We estimate the total force to be about 1,500 men so far."

A rocket-propelled grenade (RPG) is a weapon system that fires rockets equipped with a warhead that explodes. They are very dangerous for ground troops, can shoot down choppers, and also stop tanks if the correct type of warhead is used.

"We took pictures of the four men who came here yesterday and by photo ID we identified one of the men to be Abdul Aalee. He was the one with the black hat and shirt. Here are the pictures. He is a member of al-Qaida and is wanted for international terrorism crimes. The other three have no feedback on yet. We didn't get a picture of Aamir since he was with you inside the bar when the drone flew over."

The pictures were passed around and the printed

report showing that Abdul Aalee was wanted for terrorist attacks killing more than 30 people in France and blowing up the London subway killing another 40 people.

Colonel Turner said, "Sergeant Cain, thank you for the excellent report and good work. You are dismissed for now but please leave the pictures."

"Yes Sir. Thank you, Sir."

As Cain walked out of the room I said, "Wow, I knew that guy in the black hat would be trouble as he gave me the evil eye like he wanted to kill me."

Captain Sessions replied, "He probably wants to kill all of us. The question is what is he doing with your friend Aamir?"

"I have no idea but when Aamir comes I am going to ask him right up front. I know he will tell me the truth."

Colonel Turner commented, "Great Jack, but what does everyone think of the General's idea? As you know we have half of our men out on patrol in the south of the state for another two weeks. So our forces are currently made up of your 96 security people and about 200 Rangers. Our tanks should give us a big advantage over 1,500 terrorists."

"Does everyone agree to let in the women and children?"

Rick spoke up stating his true feelings, "I say we don't let any of them in Tocabaga. If one is a terrorist then they may all be terrorists."

Tommy replied, "Yes, Rick could be right, if we let them in who knows what could happen."

No one spoke for a few minutes then Jim Bo, my son-in-law, said, "How do we know we can trust the women? They can be just as dangerous as any man."

Captain Sessions replied, "Of course the women will not be let in without being searched first for any weapons. Captain Riley and perhaps Amy will be in charge of that as only women can search women.

"We will set up a tent and have each one enter to be searched without the others seeing what is going on. We will take their pictures and fingerprints and have them checked out. To check DNA it takes too long, pictures and prints we can check in a few hours, so that will have to do."

I commented, "Good idea as a woman can also carry a bomb. We need to be very careful. As for the men, we need to complete the background checks. We can't assume they are all terrorists."

Captain Sessions said, "Here is the plan. Aamir comes here today at noon we tell him our idea that the women and kids can come in Tocabaga. His group of men will help fight al-Qaida when they come. He will be on . . . THE FRONT LINE . . . but not really because our Bradley's and Abrams Tank will blow the bad guys off the map as soon as they are in sight. I don't see them getting within 200 yards of the front line. After Aamir and his men have helped us defeat al-Qaida then they have proven themselves. If all goes well we can accept them based on fingerprints and picture security checks. If we take any prisoners we will need Aamir to help with translations."

The Bradley M3 Fighting Vehicle, named after General Omar Bradley from WWII, has a three-member crew, weights 27 tons, and is fully armored. It fires a 25mm chain gun which can destroy most tanks and has a 7.62 M240 machine gun to mow down ground troops if needed. Some also have tow missiles that can blow up anything even a building.

The M1 Abrams Tank named after General Abrams, fires a whopping 120mm laser aimed cannon and never misses its target. The cannon can blow up buildings. It has one M243 50 Caliber Heavy Machine Gun, and two 7.62 M240 machine guns. Bullets and other large projectiles just bounce off the sides of this big boy.

"Jack, you need to pump Aamir for more information and feel free to tell him we already knew about al-Qaida. Ask him if he knows the guy in the black hat is Abdul Aalee a wanted terrorist."

I said, "Perhaps we should arrest him when he comes back with Aamir."

Sitting there I received an email from General Harper sent to my tocabaga.jack@gmail.com address. It read:"Jack what do you think of my plan?" I emailed back, "Colonel Turner told us, and I agree it is a good plan. We are in a meeting now discussing that, thank you."

Everyone was sitting there watching me respond to my email. No one said a word.

"I just got an email from General Harper. I told him I liked his plan."

Sessions replied, "Jack, I thought about arresting him on the spot but let's wait a while to see what he is up too."

"Okay, I agree and we will see what Aamir tells us."

Rick commented, "I say shoot him on the spot."

My brother Ron said, "I agree with Rick."

Ignoring the comments from Rick and Ron, Sessions replied, "Now let's discuss what we will do when al-Qaida attacks us. I have 200 men and I need 50 to cover and protect the Fort area. The rest will be assigned to the bridges, with about 85 to the main bridge and 10 to the south bridge."

"When the fighting starts we will have air cover from our choppers using their M134 Mini Gatling guns and 50 caliber machine guns. They will fly in from behind the enemy creating a squeeze and with no escape for al-Qaida. We are going to line the roadside with Claymore mines. I want to finish off al-Qaida once and for all. I will land 50 Rangers behind them to cut off any who try to escape."

The M134 Minigun is a 7.62x51mm NATO round and an electric operated six-barreled machine gun, which can fire up to 6,000 rounds per minute. It fires bullets so fast you can cut a telephone pole in half in a few seconds. It mows men down like a bowling ball knocking over pins leaving a bloody mess. Once this gun starts spitting fire there is no safe place to hide.

"I would like your 96 security people to cover the east and west sides of the island watching for boats. We will assign you eight M249 SAWs (squad automatic weapon) and 2 Barrett 50 caliber BMG sniper rifles. You can pick out who gets what. I suggest you break the men down into 12 man teams for a total of 8 teams. Each team will have an M240 and each man will be issued 4 hand grenades."

The 50 BMG is a 50 caliber rifle, shooting a Browning machine gun round that can go through steel, even an engine block. It can go through one side of a car, come out the other side, and kill someone. The BMG has a muzzle velocity of 1,900 miles per hour or 2,800 feet per second. The BMG bullet is a ½-inch in diameter and nearly 4 inches long. I call it the Superman Bullet.

A SAW M249 is a light machine gun that fires a 5.56 NATO round up to 700 rounds per minute. It is an awesome weapon that can be moved very quickly using a 2 man team. You need 2 men to carry all the ammo this baby fires. It is belt fed or uses 100 round drums. The effective range is 600 yards.

"The Colonel and I think we should go on high alert now and start getting the ammo and sandbags set up at the locations they are needed. Jack, it is up to you for the east and west side of the island to determine the best locations. We suggest that everyone work a 12-hour security shift. When the attack comes everyone will be on duty until the battle is over."

"Anyone have questions? Okay, if not then make it so. The Colonel and I will be roving around, making sure things are done correctly."

"Everyone is dismissed except for Jack."

"Jack, when Aamir comes bring him here to the bar right away. I think it is better that the Colonel tell him what we are willing to do. He will have no choice if he wants to save his family. What do you think?"

"Captain, I agree with you and I think he will accept our offer. If there isn't anything else Captain, I need to get my security people set up. Please have your men bring the eight M249 machine guns and the two 50 cal. Sniper rifles to the bank. I will have Ron and Tommy distribute them accordingly. I will radio you when Aamir arrives. It is almost 11am so he will be here soon."

"Okay, Jack, see you later."

"Captain, Colonel, thank you. I'll see you later."

The board and security heads were waiting outside for me. I advised Ron and Tommy to pick the teams and assign the eight M249 guns and two BMG sniper rifles as they see fit. They would assign four teams of 12 to guard the east and west side of Tocabaga. Each team would have one SAW and each side of the island would have one 50 BMG, which can shoot a mile and is a deadly weapon with the right shooter.

One of our best shooters is Tony the bar keeper. He has the eye hand coordination and is almost as good a shot as Tommy, so Tony will man one of the 50 caliber sniper rifles and Handyman Chris will man the big gun on the east side of the island, he is also a deadly shot.

We were starting our 12-hour watch duty immediately. Everyone was given the order to shoot anything moving in the water. "Shoot first ask questions later" is my motto.

I asked Tommy and Ron to meet me at the bridge at noon. I wanted Tommy and Ron to stick near me if and when the shit hits the fan.

I went home and told Hemmi, Amy, and Tonya, my son's wife, what happened at the meeting. I told them we are now on high alert and we would be doing 12-hour security details. I also advised them to stay close to home with the kids, Kendra and Shanda. I asked them to keep their guns handy and lock all the doors and shutters. Don't open the door for anyone unless you can see who it is, if it is someone you don't know shoot first and ask questions later.

I asked everyone to pass on the word that we were on high alert and to be ready for anything. Rick put up a notice on the community bulletin board. Rick would be in command of the west side and Jim Bo in command of the east side of the island.

I was at the bridge along with Tommy and Ron when Aamir arrived. It was the same old car and there were four people. Aamir got out and to my surprise so did Rahim, the two of them started to walk up the bridge when a Ranger stopped them. We went down to see what the problem was. While walking down to them I looked to see if Abdul was with them but he was not.

I asked, "What is the problem, Ranger Kelly?"

The Ranger replied, "These men don't have ID badges to enter Camp Tocabaga."

I stepped a few feet away and got on the radio to Captain Sessions, "Captain, please advise Ranger Kelly to let two people pass as they are our guests. A man named Rahim is with Aamir. I know him and he can be trusted. Oh, by the way Abdul did not show up."

Sessions cleared up the problem with Ranger

Kelly and then Rahim came up and gave me a big bear hug, like he always did in the past.

"Rahim, it is great to see you. I am very happy you came to this meeting with Aamir. I would like you to meet my son Tommy and brother Ron."

Rahim stuck out his big hand and shook hands with everyone and said with an accent, "It is my pleasure and honor to meet both of you."

Tommy and Ron both commented, "It is nice to meet you Rahim."

Aamir stepped forward and said, "Hello Tommy and Ron. It is nice to meet Jack's brother."

Ron replied, "It is nice to meet you Aamir," and they shook hands.

I said, "Okay, introductions are over, let's go to the meeting. The Colonel is waiting for us."

We walked into the bar where Colonel Turner and Captain Sessions were seated at a table. There were only three chairs left at the table so Aamir, Rahim, and I sat down. Ron and Tommy sat at the bar.

"Colonel Turner and Captain Sessions, this is Rahim a mutual friend of ours. I have known Rahim for about 10 years."

Standing up everyone shook hands and Rahim said, "I am here to help Aamir in any way possible so there are no misunderstandings."

Colonel Turner replied, "Rahim, thank you for coming."

"Getting down to business, we have agreed to allow your wives and children to come into Camp Tocabaga to live as long as they'd like. We will assign housing for them and a few people, like Jack's wife, we'll see they are made at home here. They will be issued ID tags, have ID pictures taken, and finger prints. Of course, before coming into the Camp they will need to be searched in private by two of our women to make sure there are no weapons or bombs."

"Now as for the men in your group we are asking you to house temporarily at the base of the bridge in tents until we can check everyone out. But we also are asking you to fight for us against al-Qaida when they come. We will set up a defensive position for your group and provide you any necessary weapons. Fighting with us provides the proof that we are on the same side."

"You will be on . . . THE FRONT LINE . . . but not really because our Bradley's and Abrams will blow the enemy off the map as soon as they are in sight. I don't see them getting within 200 yards of the front line. Anyone have any questions or comments?"

Aamir starts to speak Arabic to Rahim, but Rahim tells him, "Aamir, speak English so everyone knows what is being said. If we are to move here then everyone will need to speak and learn better English.

For us to speak in Arabic is not polite and could make problems."

Aamir replies, "I am very sorry and Rahim is correct. It is sometimes hard to express myself quickly in English but I will try. So our women and children can come in right away. Is that correct, Colonel Turner?"

"Yes that is correct as soon as you bring them here."

"Then you want my men to live in tents until we are cleared and to fight al-Qaida when they come. My question is how long to clear us men."

"As I told you before possibly up to one month; we need DNA samples, pictures and finger prints."

"That is too long to be without our wives."

"You can see your wives and children anytime as they can go in and out of the Camp whenever they like. We will give you radios to contact your wives. They will bring your food, do your laundry, and so forth. If al-Qaida attacks us before your clearance and your men serve with honor then we will waive the waiting time."

Rahim said, "That sounds good to me Aamir. Jack's wife and daughter will help watch our women and children. They can come out of the Camp and visit us all day."

After a very long pause, Aamir commented, "Okay, I agree with Rahim. We will do this."

I said, "Great but we have some questions to ask you both and some information to tell you. First of all, how do you know about al-Qaida, and who told you?"

Aamir sat there for a minute or two and then replied, "My brother-in-law Abdul Aalee. He was here yesterday wearing the black hat and shirt. He knows all about al-Qaida for some reason. He is very smart and has many contacts."

"Why didn't he come here today?"

"Because Rahim came with me and there was no room in the car and he did not want to anyway."

"Well I don't know how to tell you this but you have a spy among you, and it is Abdul Aalee. He is a member of al-Qaida. Here is his wanted picture for terrorist attacks in London and France, he has killed 70 people."

"I don't know what to say he never told us he was in al-Qaida. We thought he just had some friends that he got information from."

Rahim said, "Shit, Abdul is al-Qaida. That is terrible, just terrible."

Colonel Turner said, "He is a key man in the al-Qaida organization here in the USA. He was using you to get to us here. If they control this area then they can obtain more guns, supplies, and have a good base to operate out of."

I asked Aamir, "Does he have any wife, kids, or any other close friends?"

"No wife, no kids, but he does have two close friends in our group who he hangs around with all the time. They have wives but no kids yet. I always thought it was strange as he was not close to me or his sister, my wife. In addition he and his friends smoke at lot of pot everyday, which I do not like. So his friends may be members of al-Qaida also. His two friends are waiting at the car now; their names are Abdullah and Abdul Hakeem."

I asked, "Are they the same people that came here yesterday?"

"No they did not come here yesterday."

Captain Sessions phoned Sergeant Cain to have the drone take new pictures of the people standing at the car waiting for Aamir to return. To check them would take about 1 to 10 hours.

I asked, "Does anyone have any ideas, what we should do now?"

Colonel Turner replied, "Yes, Aamir, how soon can you come back with your group and when do you think al-Qaida will attack?"

"We can come back tomorrow by 10am. We

need time to pack up our stuff. As far as when al-Qaida could attack I would guess within the next 2 to 5 days. I base this on what Abdul told me. He was pushing for us to move here in 3 days. Abdul thought he would be coming in the camp yesterday and he found out he could not; he was upset. He asked me many questions: how many people are here, what type of guns you have, and so forth."

I commented, "That is a key point Abdul Aalee and the other two men were trying to get into our camp and help al-Qaida from the inside by shooting us in the back or something during the battle. They are using Aamir and Rahim to get into our camp."

Turner replied, "Okay, Aamir and Rahim bring your group here by 10am. We will be waiting for you. When you arrive, we will arrest Abdul Aalee, Abdul Hakeem, and Abdullah on the spot. Abdul Aalee we know is a terrorist but the other two we will hold until a security check is done. When you return home act normal and do not reveal our trap. Hopefully these three men will return with your group to Camp Tocabaga."

"To arrest these guys is going to be tricky without anyone getting hurt. I suggest that Jack, Tommy, and Ron do it because if any of my Rangers get close to them it may cause a problem."

"Aamir and Rahim, is there any way to get all three of them to ride in one car?"

Aamir replied, "Yes, they will want to do that and I will be the driver."

"Okay, fine. What is the color of the car?"

"It is a dark blue Chevy."

Turner stressed, "Listen carefully, Aamir, you will be the first car to pull up. Jack you arrest Abdul Aalee, Ron gets Abdullah, and Tommy can arrest Abdul Hakeem. If there is any resistance use deadly force to protect yourself."

"As soon as everyone is out of the car Jack will come over and shake your hand Aamir, so be standing next to Abdul Aalee when this happens. This is the signal. As soon as Jack lets go of your hand, Jack, Ron, and Tommy draw your weapons and tell them they are under arrest. Hold them at gun point until my men move in. My Rangers will read them their rights and don't worry my Rangers will cover your backs."

"Does everyone agree with this plan?"

I said, "How about a verbal signal be used instead so Tommy and Ron don't have to watch my hand? What about this, after I shake your hand I will say welcome to Camp Tocabaga. As soon as I say Tocabaga we draw our weapons and Aamir gets out of the way fast because I think Abdul Aalee is going to fight to the death."

Turner replied, "Yes, a verbal signal is better . . . so after you shake hands you will say welcome to Camp Tocabaga. On the word Tocabaga you draw your weapons. Everyone got that?"

Everyone replied, "Yes."

Rahim commented, "I think you will need to arrest their wives also as they cannot be trusted. They would kill for their husbands."

"You can point out their wives after we arrest the men. I think that concludes our meeting. Are there any questions or comments?"

No one replied.

Captain Sessions said, "Thank you Gentlemen for your kind help and support. We are all safer and better off working together to protect our American way of life."

Everyone shook hands and I took Aamir and Rahim back to the bridge. It was about 4pm.

As usual Aamir said, "Peace be with you."

"Peace be with both of you and be careful my friends. I will see you at 10am."

I watched them all get in the old car and leave. I hoped that Aamir and Rahim would be careful because if al-Qaida finds out what is going on, they would kill them and their families.

Then I had brainstorm idea. I radioed Captain Sessions and asked him to have a drone follow Abdul

Aalee tonight as he may lead us to the al-Qaida headquarters. He may go there tonight to tell them he will be going to Tocabaga. It will be necessary for the drone to follow Aamir home first to find Abdul Aalee. Captain Sessions thought this was a good idea.

MAY 12, 2025

I received a phone call from Captain Sessions at 7am.

"Jack, Abdullah and Abdul Hakeem are both wanted for terrorism attacks committed in Ohio. They robbed and killed several people and beheaded two men, last year. So they are very dangerous people, it appears Aamir, and Rahim don't know it."

"More important news is we did follow Abdul Aalee last night and found out where the al-Qaida head quarters may be located. It is located at an old Church on 54th Ave. South about five miles from here. He went there around midnight and stayed for about 2 hours. After we arrest them today we may do a raid on that location. We will need approval from General Harper. The Colonel is on the line with him right now."

"Captain Sessions thank you for your good work. Now we know these three guys are all dirt bags and if we shoot them it will be justified. I will let Tommy and Ron know. I will see you at the bridge at around 9:30."

Tommy, Ron, and the whole family were sleeping at my house, considered the safe house due to the metal shutters I had installed years ago. We had some time so we ate some breakfast and I told everyone the news I received from Captain Sessions. This news made our job easier as now we knew the three guys were dirty terrorists and we wouldn't mind killing them on the spot.

I got another brainstorm idea. If that church is their headquarters then maybe they have hidden some gold, silver, or money there. They need funds, some kind of cash to pay for their travel, food, clothes, guns, or whatever they need. Of course most of what they need they steal and kill to obtain it. These guys have been robbing banks, people, and stores for a couple of years. But maybe, just maybe, there is a gold treasure to be found. I will tell Tommy and Ron about my idea later.

At 9am we are at the bridge waiting for Aamir and his group to show up. This is a very dangerous situation. No one knows what is going to happen; no one knows what Abdul Aalee is going to do. I suspect that he will fight to the death like other extremists do rather than be taken prisoner.

Captain Sessions showed up at 9:30 as promised. He advised us that he would have five Rangers covering the entire group, watching our backs when we arrest the terrorists. We reviewed the plan once again so everyone understood what to do and when. When Aamir arrives the three bad guys will be in his car. Once they all get out of the car Tommy, Ron, and I will approach them, I will shake Aamir's hand, and when I let go of the hand shake I will say, "Welcome to Tocabaga." As soon as I say "Tocabaga" we all draw our weapons and tell the terrorists not to move. Then the Rangers move in and take any weapons they may have, and lead them to the guard house located at the Fort.

It sounds easy but a million things can go wrong. I am worried and I have told Tommy and Ron to shoot if anyone makes a slight move. You need to shoot first or you could be killed. The bad guys don't care if they die because they believe a better life is waiting for them in never never land.

I decided to change the key word to use as the signal to draw our weapons.

I advised everyone I would say, "Hello friends, welcome to Tocabaga." We draw our weapons on the word "Hello." I changed this just in case Abdul Aalee found out our plan somehow from Aamir or Rahim.

Tommy yelled, "Here they come!"

Looking down the road I saw four cars coming, my hands started to sweat so I wiped them off on my pants. I told Ron and Tommy get ready, check your Glock, and make sure there is a round in the chamber. Stay close to me. Everyone in my family has a Glock 9mm hand gun.

A Glock is without a doubt the best hand gun ever made. The barrels never wear out and they are very dependable. It will fire under water, you can throw it in the mud or run it over with a truck, and it still works every time. It is light weight and has a 15 to 17 round magazine capacity, which means you can fire a lot of bullets. I like the luger 9mm round because it is the most common hand gun ammunition. It is used by the military and police departments all over the United States.

The cars pulled up to the bottom of the bridge and stopped. I turned around to check if the Rangers were in position. We walked up to the blue Chevy and Aamir got out and so did the Abdul Aalee and the other two bad guys. Tommy was on my right side. Ron was next to Tommy. Aamir walked around the car and stepped up to me to shake hands, while the three terrorists watched standing a little behind Aamir, to the right side of him.

As Aamir was putting his hand out to shake mine, I looked at Abdul Aalee. I had a clear shot. Tommy had a clear shot at Abdul Hakeem, but Ron didn't have a clear shot as Abdullah was standing almost behind Aamir. I saw out of the corner of my eye Ron move slightly to his left, maybe that move would give him a clear shot. It seemed as if time slowed down.

Aamir's hand was hanging in mid-air waiting for me to shake his hand. I raised my arm while looking at Abdul Aalee to see if he had a gun. I saw none. I glanced back to Aamir and our hands touched.

I said, "Hello friends, welcome to Tocabaga."

As I said, "Hello" I quickly pulled my hand back and drew my Glock 17 pointing it directly at Abdul Aalee. I yelled, "Don't anyone move you are under arrest. Raise your hands!"

I didn't look. I didn't dare take my eyes off Abdul, but I could feel that Tommy and Ron had their targets covered. Aamir quickly moved out of the way, getting behind us.

The look on Abdul's face was one of anger. He slowly started to raise his hands but he suddenly reached behind his back to pull out a hand gun while he was screaming something in Arabic. That was all I needed to see and I shot him twice in the chest.

I quickly glanced at the other two. They just stood there, not making a move, with their hands in the air. Looking back at Abdul laying on the ground he didn't move, so I walked over to him, bending down to pick up his gun and check if he had a pulse.

Suddenly I felt his hand grab my throat, his thumb was pressing directly below my Adam's apple, and it was choking me. He had both hands on my neck. Our faces were close together; I could smell his stinking hot breath.

I had no choice but to put my gun to his head and pull the trigger…BAM…blowing his brains out all over the road and spraying my face with warm red blood. The gun blast caused my ears to ring. I couldn't hear for a few minutes.

I ripped opened his shirt and he had on a bulletproof vest; my two shots to his chest only knocked him down stunning him. I was a stupid shit and should have done a triple tap, one bullet to the head and two in the chest.

I took a deep breath trying to control my heart rate and calm down. My hands were shaking as I put my gun back into the holster and stood up in relief. My knees were shaking and I almost fell down, so I sat down on the side of the road.

Four Rangers came up from behind us and frisked Abdullah and Abdul Hakeem, finding a gun on both of them. They put plastic ties on their wrists telling them you are under arrest for terrorist acts against the United States. Neither one said a word.

Tommy came up to me and asked, "Are you okay?"

"Yeah, I just need to get my breath back. That guy choked the shit out of me. He was a strong little bastard."

"Here take this wet towel and wipe the blood off your face. I had you covered, Dad. I was just getting ready to shoot him in the head myself but you beat me to it."

"I know. Thanks, Tommy."

Two women ran up begging the Rangers not to take their husbands away. Aamir told the two women their husbands were members of al-Qaida and that Abdul Aalee was their leader. The women started to wail as their husbands were taken away. Speaking in Arabic, they told Aamir they had no idea that their husbands were in al-Qaida. Aamir believed them but I did not. The Rangers took them aside and had Captain

Riley search them for weapons but none were found.

I looked at the rest of the group and Rahim, they were standing there with their hands up.

I yelled to Rahim, "It is okay, everyone put your hands down."

I waved for them to come closer.

Captain Sessions came over to me and commented, "Jack, good job you did what you had to do. I saw the whole thing happen. It was a justified shooting."

I just gave him a knuckle bump, as I didn't want to talk about it. I felt sick for some reason; maybe I needed a shot of whiskey and a beer. Yes, that would take the edge off but there was still a lot of work to do helping our new friends get moved in.

Captain Sessions asked Aamir, "Please bring your people together for a meeting to explain what is going to happen."

Aamir called everyone to the base of the bridge, a total of twenty people with six kids under the age of ten, six men and eight women. The first thing the Captain did was to ask everyone to hand in his or her cell phones.

Since 2012, the NSA (National Security Agency) has been collecting phone and internet data. Your phone number is like your ID number; they can check every call you made and every call that you received over the years. So this is another way to do a background check.

As Captain Sessions was talking, the Rangers were setting up two tents and a canopy on the small beach about 300 feet away. These were not normal tents as they had hard side walls and small generators to power air conditioning and provide electric power. These were the living quarters for the six men until their background checks were done. It looked like a campground and they even had a latrine installed.

The Rangers put up walls of sand bags near the tents, on both sides of the road, to create a "V" shaped defensive firing line. In addition, I noticed they were mounting Claymore mines on the inside and outside of the guard rails along the side of road.

Internally a M18A1 Claymore mine contains C4 explosives and a layer of seven hundred $\frac{1}{8}$-inch-diameter steel balls set into an epoxy resin. When it is detonated, the explosion drives the steel balls forward, out of the mine. The steel balls are projected in a 60-degree fan-shaped pattern that is 6.5 feet high and 55 yards wide at a range of 150 feet. A very effective killing weapon because one mine can kill or wound many men.

Amy and Captain Riley went to talk to the

Muslim women and give them ID tags, after they were checked for weapons in the privacy of a tent. Everyone was talking and seemed happy to be here except for the two women whose husbands were arrested. The other women seemed to be ignoring them, and they looked like they were in shock, they needed help.

Amy and Captain Riley were moving them into their new homes. The wives of Abdullah and Abdul Hakeem moved into one house by themselves as they were terrorist suspects. The other six women moved into another house. They didn't want to have the terrorist wives living with them. They were being shunned because of what their husbands did.

Seeing Captain Sessions, I asked, "Is it okay if we take the men to see where their wives are living? You know just show them around a little so they don't feel like prisoners."

"Yes it's okay but they can't bring any guns into Camp Tocabaga and I would like you to be with them at all times. First, see Sergeant Smith and obtain DNA samples, pictures, and fingerprints so we can get the security checks started. Actually, they can come in anytime they like as long as you or one of your people are with them at all times until they receive their clearance."

"Okay, Captain. Thank you, that will make them feel a lot better knowing their wives have good living accommodations."

"Jack, we will post a security guard outside their

house 24-7 just in case some of them want to roam around at night. We are also going to question and interrogate Abdullah and Abdul Hakeem. We need to find out more information."

"Sounds like a good idea to me, it's also for their safety. Captain, interrogate the hell out of them."

"Yes, it is for everyone's safety. Are you going to take care of the body?"

"Yes, I have to talk to Aamir and Rahim about that, so see you later."

Now we had to deal with body of Abdul Aalee. Aamir advised it was ok to bury him at sea. He and some of his men wrapped the body in plain white cloth and placed it in a body bag with bricks to help it sink. Loading the body on a boat, Rahim went with Rick and Chris to say the proper prayers when they lowered the body into the deep dark water. I would have just fed him to the sharks.

It was getting late; dusk was coming. Ron and I took Aamir, Rahim, and the other four men inside the Camp to visit their wives and see their living conditions. They were pleased to see that all was okay and we returned to the tents.

Arriving at the tents, Colonel Turner and Captain Sessions were standing there with 12 Rangers.

Sessions said, "Everyone pay attention, we have lined the road with Claymore mines along the guard rails, which will be activated when we see the enemy coming. They operate on motion sensors. So no one should go down the road after the mines are hot or activated, otherwise you will be blown to shit. If you do not understand this say so now. If you hear a Claymore blow that means the enemy is here, so be alert."

All was quiet, no one replied.

"In addition I will have 12 Rangers here on THE FRONT LINE with Aamir and his men. My Rangers will be located on the other side of the road, in a so-called machine gun nest. If al-Qaida attacks we are ready. If anyone has any questions speak up now."

Aamir said, "Are you going to give us guns to use? We only have two hand guns."

"Of course, Sergeant Kelly will pass out a new rifle to each of you and 500 rounds of ammunition tomorrow. Does everyone know how to use a M 4 or AR 15?"

Rahim was the only one to reply. "No I never shot a gun before. I do not like guns because I do not like killing people."

Sergeant Kelly said, "Okay, then you can be an ammunition runner and re-loader for your group."

"What is that job?"

"It is simple you just run back to the bridge and carry ammo back as it is needed to your guys. Don't let them run out of ammo."

"Okay, I will do my best for the group."

Sessions said, "If nothing else, carry on and get ready. Your tents are all set up to use."

Tommy, Ron, Jim Bo, and I walked back to the bridge with Sessions and Turner.

Turner commented, "These guys don't know shit, so keep your eye on them, Jack, or they could all get killed when the bullets start to fly."

I said, "Let's go get a shot and a beer. I need it bad."

Arriving at the bar no one was there, Tony was on guard duty so we just helped ourselves to the booze.

I commented, "My neck still hurts from that little bastard choking me today. So this shot of JD may help me relax. I think I'll have a double."

We all raised our shot glasses and Colonel Turner said, "To Freedom and the Constitution."

We all repeated the toast together and clinked glasses . . . we felt like a band of brothers. Actually, we have all wanted to even the score with al-Qaida. It is one battle we are looking forward to.

Sessions said, "I got to go check on how the interrogation is going."

Turner replied, "I got to report to the General, stay alert."

We shook hands, and they left the bar. I had another round of drinks and went home for dinner, which was well deserved since we had nothing to eat all day. I was bushed, smelled from sweating all day, and needed a hose shower.

I had no sooner cleaned up and ate my dinner when I received a call on my Army cell phone from Captain Sessions. It was 10pm.

"Jack, listen up, the two terrorists talked and told us everything they knew, we think. Also we received finger print analysis back on Aamir and his group along with photo identification analysis. NSA phone checks also came in. Guess what we found out?"

"Captain, I have no idea, but nothing would surprise me."

"We found out all of them are al-Qaida members except for Rahim. He is the only one that has no record."

"Are you sure about that?"

"Yes, I double checked finger prints, phone logs, face recognition methods, and all of them show up multiple times as al-Qaida related. There is no mistake."

"How did you make Abdullah and Abdul Hakeem talk?"

"We used a little pig's blood and a knife."

"You don't have any pig blood."

"We used chicken blood and told them it was pig blood and they were going to drink it. Then we sharpened a knife and told them we would cut off their most important body part so they couldn't use it in the next world. That scared the shit out of them. Of course we weren't going to do anything to them."

"What about the women are they in al-Qaida?"

"Sorry to say, it's the same for the women. The NSA has phone records of communications to al Qaida, except for Rahim's wife. She has no record. I don't know what to do with them other than keep them under guard. The Colonel is talking to General Harper about the situation. I have notified my front line to keep a close watch on Aamir. It's a good thing we didn't give them any guns yet."

"I also ordered the Claymore mines to be activated now so if any of them try to sneak down the road they will set off the Claymore mines. We will arrest Aamir and the whole group at 0800 hours tomorrow."

"One more thing, our drones have seen hundreds of men going into the four condo buildings over the last 24 hours which means they are using that as a staging area. Tomorrow we will have Iron Maiden blow up those buildings in a preemptive strike. Meet me at the bridge at 0700 hours. Tell your men to be on high alert and inform them of the situation."

"At 0730, you tell Rahim that his wife wants to see him and take him up the bridge, and then my men will disarm Aamir and his men hopefully without a shot."

"The plan is our Armor vehicles will open fire at 0745 hours. My hope is that Aamir and his group will be distracted by this while my Rangers sneak up behind them. My Rangers will be pretending to watch the fireworks. It will be noisy and smoky when the big guns start to fire, at 0800 hours the guns stop and my Rangers will make their move."

"Yes Sir, Captain, thank you for the update see you at 7am."

Putting down the phone I told my whole family (Tommy, Ron, Jim Bo, Amy, Tonya, and Hemmi) what Sessions had reported to me. They could not believe it either, we just sat there for a few minutes, and no one knew what to say.

Tommy said in a loud voice, "Damn, what a bunch of liars! See I told you Dad I didn't trust Aamir."

I thought what a big pile of shit this turned out to be. Tommy was right I should have gone with my gut instincts about Aamir. What are we going to do with the

six little kids after everyone is arrested or killed?
Rahim and his wife are in great danger and they don't
know it. I won't be able to sleep tonight thinking about
what could happen tomorrow.

MAY 13, 2025

All of us that were not on guard duty were at the bridge at 7am, which means 32 men all armed to the teeth plus 75 Rangers. Everyone knew the plan.

I grabbed two cups of coffee and walked up to Rahim handing him one and said, "Good Morning."

The others looked at me and said nothing, they were drinking some kind of tea. Looking at my watch it was 0740 hours.

Rahim said, "Good Morning, Jack, thanks for the coffee."

"Rahim your wife wants to see you. She thinks your little girl is sick. Come on I will take you to her."

The others looked at us as we walked away and Rahim told them, "I will be back soon. I need to check on my little girl."

As we reached the top of the bridge it was 0745 and the Iron Maiden let loose with its 120mm cannon . . . KABOOM . . . scaring the shit out of Aamir and his men. I stood there with Rahim; he looked shocked and dropped his cup of coffee. KABOOM . . . KABOOM . . . KABOOM . . . the Iron Maiden was firing like crazy.

Every time it fired, everyone jumped, as it was loud as hell. A shock wave or pressure wave blew over everyone, knocking off my hat off. You had to cover your ears for fear your eardrums would be blown out.

When the Abrams fired it shook the whole ground around you, and the big tank seemed to jump in the air with sand and dust blowing making a big cloud.

Looking down the road you could see the smoke and dust rising in the air from the buildings. Now the Predator and Gun Smoke started to fire their 25mm Bushmaster chain guns.

Bushmaster chain guns fire a 25mm round which is about 1 inch in diameter at a rate of 200 to 500 rounds per minute. It has an effective range of 1.5 miles.

I looked down at Aamir and his men they were holding their ears and looking down the road at the smoke and dust in the air. The rangers were now right behind them, within 15 feet. Suddenly the firing stopped and the Rangers yelled, "Freeze, drop your weapons and raise your hands."

Aamir didn't even have a gun in his hand, and yelled, "What the hell are you doing?"

Sergeant Kelly yelled, "You are all under arrest for terrorism and related acts."

Aamir and his bad boys darted for the blue Chevy just a few feet away. No one fired a shot at them as they could not get away. Jumping into the car they started to drive quickly down the road, we all just stood there watching, knowing the Claymore mines were going to kill them all. Aamir either forgot about the mines or thought they were not activated.

The Chevy was few hundred feet away when the first two Claymore mines went off . . . BOOM . . . sending 1400 bullet like projectiles ripping through the Chevy. Glass and metal where flying off the car in small pieces. I knew they all had to be dead, but the car kept rolling even with flat tires and two more mines blew up, starting the car on fire. It was a burning wreck with black smoke billowing into the blue sky.

I said out loud, "Peace be with you, Aamir."

Rahim looked at me said, "Yes, Peace be with you, Aamir. What just happen Jack?"

I told Rahim, "Your kid is fine. I told you that to get you away from Aamir and the others. You are the only one who passed the security check. Aamir and the others all had records and didn't pass the security check including their wives. They are all members of al-Qaida."

Rahim replied, "I never really knew that but I did have a feeling he did not like people who didn't believe in Islam. I don't know what to say. I don't even know my own people."

"There is nothing to say my friend. Aamir killed himself. If he didn't most likely he would have faced a firing squad for the crimes he committed. You don't have anything to worry about; you and your wife have a security clearance. The problem we have now is what to do with their wives and kids.

"Rahim, I can't believe that Aamir would put his wife and kid in a dangerous situation. Did he really want his family here for protection? We will never know now I guess."

"Right, Jack, we will never know what Aamir or who Aamir really is."

"Jack, I know these women. They are no threat. They would never attack or kill anyone. Yes, maybe they made phone calls for their husbands or did something for them but I really don't think they would hurt any person. I will take them all under my wing and be responsible for them."

"I have one idea and that is to take them to the Islamic Society in Tampa, if the Army will let them go. It is better they be with people with the same thinking. I have a friend who works there and if you give me back my phone I could call him. There are over 20 mosques in the Tampa area and they are well protected."

"Over twenty, I never knew there were so many. I think the Army will be happy to let them go as they don't know what to do with women and children. The problem is how do we take them there? It's over 40 miles away. Maybe Colonel Turner will let us use a chopper. I forgot we still have your phone."

"Ok, Rahim let's talk to the Captain about this later. The Rangers are going to attack al-Qaida so let's find out how we can help."

Colonel Turner ordered his men to mount up, which meant get ready to move out, there were five Hummers and five big trucks. A total of 75 Rangers with two Bradleys, and the Iron Maiden headed down the road to the smoking condos. They were going to mop up or kill any al-Qaida still around or still alive. Ten Black Hawk helicopters flew overhead toward the destroyed condominiums.

I asked Sessions, "What can we do to help?"

Sessions told me, "Jack, stay alert here I don't know when we will return. I am leaving 12 Rangers here on the front line. The mines are turned off now but Sergeant Kelly has the switch to activate them if necessary."

"Yes Sir, Captain, will do. Captain, before you go Rahim came up with an idea on what to do with the Muslim women and children. If we let them go, the Islamic Society in Tampa would take them in. Rahim has a friend living there and he would call him to confirm it. If you and the Colonel agree we would need a chopper to take them there."

"Jack, right now I can't spare any choppers and don't have time to discuss what will happen to the women. After this battle, I will make time to meet with you and Rahim to discuss the subject."

"Ok thank you, Captain, sorry about my bad timing. Good hunting, stay safe."

As the Captain jumped into his Hummer, I

shook his hand. He didn't say a word; he just looked at all of us standing there and then saluted us, telling his driver, "Let's go."

Rick, Tommy, Eddie, Ron, Rahim, and I stood there and watched the convoy rumble down the road, driving around the still burning blue Chevy containing the charred bodies of Aamir and his cohorts. We were all worried about the Rangers and what would happen, how many would die or be wounded in the upcoming battle.

I picked up my radio telling everyone, "Be on alert. The Rangers have gone to mop up what is left of al-Qaida."

About 20 minutes went by and we heard the Iron Maiden basting away again along with the rapid fire of the 25mm chain guns. We stood there looking down the road hoping and praying for our men. Men we have come to know as friends, good friends, men who think like we do, loyal to the US Constitution.

I told Rahim, "Come on I will take you to your wife and kid. On the way we will stop at my house and pick up three security badges, you need to wear them at all times. Tommy and Ron, I will be back soon."

I moved Rahim and his family to another vacant condo so they could be alone.

I told Rahim, "You and your wife can come and go as you please. I am moving all the women into the unit next door. Maybe you could talk to them and get them some food if they are hungry."

I doubled the guard advising them that Rahim and his wife can come to visit. Driving back to the bridge I could still hear cannon fire coming from Iron Maiden. I guess Captain Riley is giving them hell.

My radio hissed, "Ten or so boats coming on the east side. This is Tony.''

Then I heard Chris, "We got about 15 small boats on the west side just coming into view."

I got on the radio, "Start shooting those damn boats, shoot the boats, and shoot the people in them. No one gets on shore."

Tommy commented, "We better keep an eye on the road if 100 bad guys get past the Rangers somehow, we got problems. Maybe we should make the Claymores hot."

"If you see anyone sneaking up the road tell Sergeant Kelly to activate the Claymore mines right away. Use your Cobb 50 and fire a superman bullet at them."

As mentioned before, the Cobb 50 BMG is a 50 caliber rifle, shooting a Browning machine gun round that can go through steel, even an engine block. It can go through one side of a car, or boat, come out the other side, and kill someone. The BMG has a muzzle velocity of 1,900 miles per hour or 2,800 feet per second. The BMG bullet is ½ inch in diameter and nearly 4 inches long. I call it the Superman Bullet. The Cobb is a semi automatic rifle, built just like an AR 15 but bigger and has a ten round magazine.

It was 10:15am when Rick, Eddie, and I grabbed our rifles and jumped in my truck heading to the west side of the island first to see what was going on. I drove to the center position where Tony was located. He was shooting a 50 caliber Sniper rifle in rapid order. Shooting boats was just like shooting plastic ducks at a shooting gallery. Tony had already sunk about half of them.

Tony said while laughing his ass off, "This is just like a video game."

Rick replied, "Keep up the good work, Tony. Watch for swimmers, and gun them down also."

I went up and down the line, talking to each 6 man team. Each team had a SAW or light machine gun. I advised them to watch for swimmers. Let no one get ashore.

It seemed all was under control on the west side of our island so we drove to the east side of the island and found that most of the boats had by passed Chris and his 50 caliber and were coming in the south at shark channel which now only had ten Rangers guarding it and they were under heavy fire. I guessed about 10 boats had made it into shark channel and some were pulling up to the docks and the scumbags were jumping on shore. There were about 50 men coming ashore.

As we ducked behind some sand bags, Sergeant Smith yelled, "RPG," which means an incoming rocket propelled grenade and everyone ducked down low. It zoomed over our heads and exploded somewhere behind us. No one was hurt. I radioed for one SAW to be moved to the south bridge right away as we needed more fire power. We lined up next to the Rangers and started shooting as many jerks as we could.

It sounds crazy but we all started to laugh. We were laughing so hard we couldn't aim straight. I had to put my rifle down several times as I was laughing so hard.

Sergeant Smith laughing said, "Why are we laughing? We could all be killed. I got two more."

Eddie laughing said, "This is fun and we are getting some payback for 9-11."

Rick yelled, "I just got two."

Eddie was right it felt good getting payback after all these years, but I think we were laughing to hide our fear of being killed or shot.

I yelled while laughing, "Shut up assholes and keep shooting."

Rangers who were guarding the Fort must have heard the gunfire and radioed us that they were in the trees covering the docks. Gunfire started coming from the tree line on the other side of shark channel in what we call NO MANS LAND. We had the enemy in an "L" shape cross fire and for them, it was the end.

The SAW machine gun arrived and David set it up. He started mowing down bad guys left and right. Some made it off the boats but none of them made it very far. Bodies laid everywhere, on the docks, on the shore, and in the water. The sharks were going to have a feast. We don't call it shark channel for nothing. We need to feed the fish now.

We call David "Dancing Dave", he is a retired insurance salesman. Of course he got his name because he loves to dance and he is good at it. But Dave has other talents he has a good shooting eye and is always thinking. Looking at him, with his short hair cut you would think he was an Army Captain. Dave never served in the Army. He always seems serious about everything but once you break the ice with him after a few drinks he does have a good sense of humor. The main point about Dave is that you can trust him.

Shark Channel is full of sharks of all kinds: Bull Sharks, Hammerhead Sharks, Black Tip Sharks, Mako Sharks, Tiger Sharks, and Lemon Sharks. Years ago, not far from here, a Great White shark was caught weighing over 500 pounds.

The gun fire slowly subsided, all the boats were sunk, and not one bad guy was moving. When it seemed safe, we walked over the south bridge to NO MANS LAND and met the ten Rangers who were helping us out. We checked the bodies laying there to make sure they were all dead by shooting them each several times. We were up close to these assholes and Eddie didn't like this part, he didn't like shooting people who were already dead, for some reason. He wasn't laughing any more.

Suddenly, Eddie yelled, "Help!"

I turned my head and saw a terrorist had Eddie on the ground and was going to shoot him. Somehow he knocked Eddie down and was getting ready to fire. He racked his AK 47. I heard the trigger snap but the gun didn't fire, lucky for Eddie. The terrorist pulled back the breach again and I saw the unfired bullet eject flying thru the air. He was placing the gun to his shoulder, moving his finger to the trigger, I needed to act fast, but it seemed I was in slow motion.

I raised my AR15 carbine to my shoulder, carefully took aim through my scope at his head about 50 feet away and fired . . . BAM . . . BAM . . . two shots in the head, the top of his head blew off, his body went limp and he fell on top of Eddie. I never miss a target that close. I shot him in the head because I was worried he might have on a bulletproof vest.

Eddie pushed the body off and stood up with blood all over him saying, "I just shit my pants."

I told Eddie, "Next time, wear your Depends, dumb shit. How did that guy knock you down?"

"I thought I saw him move so I walked over closer and then he kicked my feet out from under me."

"Damn Eddie, don't stand there and look at them, shoot them right away or you could get killed! Don't get so close to the bodies. Shoot them in the head just like they are zombies. That guy had on a vest."

Rick was laughing at Eddie and said, "Eddie, you are a dumb shit, be more careful and use your brain."

Eddie yelled, "It's not funny, Rick!"

When we finished shooting all the bodies, two Rangers would each grab a leg and drag them to the water, throw them in to make more fish food. Three boats got away from us and we don't know where they went. I estimated a total of 12 men got away. I was not happy about that.

Tony was on the radio, "Jack, all clear here. No one is alive that we can see, since they are all in the water."

"Tony, please have everyone shoot each floating body again to make sure they are all dead; it is good target practice. We can't take any chances of having these guys getting onto Tocabaga."

The Radio came on, "Jack, Chris here, I see 3 boats out in the deep channel out of my rifle range heading north."

"Okay, Chris, keep watching them. I will call Sergeant Cain who is in charge of the drones."

I called Sergeant Cain on my Army cell phone, "Sergeant Cain, this is Jack Gunn. I need your help to follow some boats using a drone."

"Ok Jack, where are the boats at?"

"East of here about 1.5 miles in the deep water channel that runs due north. These are al-Qaida guys and I want to see where those boats go. Don't attack them just follow them and tell me where they go."

"Roger that Jack, I'll let you know. I have a drone near that area now."

There are many types of drones; they come in many sizes from small bird types to larger ones the size of a small plane. Some of the drones carry missiles like the Predator Drone, which is used to destroy cars, boats, or people. Usually you can't see a drone or hear one due to their size and the fact they make hardly any noise flying high in the air. They are a great tool to spy on people since they can take excellent pictures and can stay in the air for many hours. Most of the information about drones is kept classified.

"I think Captain Sessions will want to know where the boats are going also. Thank you, Sergeant Cain."

Rick, Eddie, and I headed back to the bar for some drinks and food. The last few days have been very stressful making us all tired. I was wondering how Captain Sessions and his Rangers were doing. It was now 3pm and I thought we should hear some news soon.

I decided to phone Captain Sessions on the hot cell phone line, and then I got a call from Sergeant Cain, "Jack, the boats went to Eckerd College and the guys got out and went into the main auditorium."

"Thank you, Sergeant Cain."

This means some al-Qaida are at the old college campus, a big place to hide in and a dangerous place to search for bad guys. This campus is down the road about two miles from where the Rangers are now fighting. I wonder how many al-Qaida fighters are hiding there.

I stopped to see how Rahim was doing. Rahim was doing fine and so were the women and kids. They were satisfied but Rahim wanted to do some kind of work. Since he liked to cook I told him to talk to Steve our head cook. Rahim and Steve know each other so it could be a good job to keep him busy. I had just arrived home and my Army cell phone rang, it was Captain Sessions.

"Jack, we have terminated a lot of al-Qaida. I don't have a body count. We have not had anyone surrender as they fight to the death. Sergeant Cain called me about the three boats going to Eckerd College and we will go there tomorrow to mop up. The Colonel has recalled our 200 men fighting south of here as we will need them to finish the mop up operations. They should be there in a few hours. Tonight I am leaving half my men here with the Tank and Bradley fighting vehicles. We still have five big buildings to clear."

"Captain, did you have any casualties?"

"Yes, two Rangers killed and two wounded not good but not so bad considering the circumstances, but one man getting killed is one too many."

"Did you hear about the attack here today?"

"Yes I did, but to be honest I was not concerned as you had that under control."

"Well what is next, Captain?"

"Tomorrow we will finish the mop up here and at the college. At the same time we will go to the church we think is the HQ for al-Qaida. The plan is to hit them all at the same time."

"Roger that Captain, what can we do to help?"

"There is nothing you can do. Just keep up your guard and give my Rangers anything they may need in the way of food or drinks. I will be out here with my men and Colonel Harper will be going back to the Fort tonight."

"Okay Captain, sorry to hear about the Rangers

killed. If you need anything let me know."

"Thanks, Jack. See you tomorrow."

Tommy and Ron walked in my home and I told them what Sessions had relayed to me. I informed them about the battle at the south bridge, and how Eddie shit his pants.

It is dark now and I hope Captain Sessions and his men will be safe for the night. I also think there may be a lot of al-Qaida fighters at the college; that is one big area with a lot of buildings to clear. It will not be an easy job, even for the Rangers.

Then I remembered the possible gold or money that maybe hidden at the church by al-Qaida. Their stash of money used to fund their operations. Once the Rangers clear the church my plan is to go there and search for those funds to help Tocabaga. Who can I take with me?

MAY 14, 2025

I slept about four hours last night because my back was killing me. If I move a certain way it means instant pain, to relieve it I took four 500mg aspirins and two shots of Jack Daniels with a glass of water.

Jim Bo came home late last night after guard duty. Thank God there were no more attacks over night. We all woke up at 6am and could hear Iron Maiden firing the big 120mm cannon. The Ranger choppers flew overhead on the way to the battle and mop up operations. I wanted to be there with my friends to help the Rangers, but we would just get in their way.

We ate some smoked fish and fruit washing it down with Eddie's beer and went outside. A thunderstorm blew in overnight and the grass was flooding. This meant the snakes and bugs would come crawling out onto the roads to get on high ground. I hoped it would not last long but sometimes the storms come on and off all day. We headed to the main bridge to see what was going on. Trucks loaded with the 200 Rangers that came back yesterday were rolling across the bridge going to the fight.

We all yelled, "Good luck!"

The cold hard rain turned to a drizzle as we stood there watching the trucks roll passed us.

All we could do was wait, which is harder than actually being there for the fight. Rick, Tony, Eddie, and Chris came up to see what was going on. I told them what Sessions told me yesterday, then I informed them of my plan to search al-Qaida HQ for possible funds to use for Tocabaga.

I explained to all, "If the church is their headquarters then maybe they have hidden some gold, silver, or money there. They need funds, some kind of cash to pay for their travel, food, clothes, guns, or whatever they need. Of course most of what they need they steal and kill to obtain it. These people have been stealing, robbing banks, robbing people, and stores for a couple of years. But maybe, just maybe, there is a gold treasure to be found."

"We need to make a team to go search the church, eight men with two SAW machine guns. Also we need two metal detectors to search the grounds. Four men will stand guard while four of us search."

Rick asked, "What are we looking for gold, silver, or what?"

"We are looking for anything that seems unusual and then the metal detectors will be used to scan the area in question. We are looking for anything to give us a sign such as fresh dirt, a crack in the floor or ceiling, a wall that looks new, or a broken tile in the floor, anything that don't look normal. If the funds are there they must be well hidden but easy to get at for a quick removal."

"So the team will be Tommy, Eddie, Tony, Chris, Rick, Ron, Jim Bo, Rahim, and me."

Eddie said, "Rahim isn't one of us. He didn't fight with us. Why do you want to bring him? He won't even carry a gun."

"Look Rahim is one of us now. I believe he may think more like Aamir than any of us, since he knew him, giving us a better idea where to search. Anyway this isn't our money it's for everyone on Tocabaga."

"If you agree raise your hand."

Everyone quickly raised his hand, but Eddie. That surprised me, as Eddie is usually a very kind and fair person.

"Okay we need to get ready to roll as soon as the Rangers clear the Church, so get your guns and equipment ready now and loaded into two trucks."

We had just finished our meeting and Colonel Turner drove up to the bridge, stopping right next to me.

"Good morning, Jack and Rick."

I replied, "Hello Colonel, I hope this rain stops soon."

Rick asked the Colonel, "How is it going over there?"

"We will finish up by 1500 hours today if all goes well."

I asked, "Colonel you know the church that we think is the HQ for al-Qaida, well we think there maybe some type of funds hidden there. Al-Qaida money used to fund their operations and we would like your permission to go search for it after the Rangers clear it. Anything we find will go to help Tocabaga."

"Jack, that is a good idea and that sounds like something al-Qaida would do, use a church to hide their funds. I approve and will have Captain Sessions call you after our men have cleared the church."

"Ok thank you, Colonel."

"No problem, Jack. I have to go now, good luck."

The colonel drove away with his four security guards toward the battlegrounds. We all knew what to do and everyone started to make ready for the big search.

We all sat down at the bar and I drew a map of the Church and the surrounding grounds. We made a plan, a search and security plan so everyone knew where to go and what to do. We were all set.

I trusted the men going with me; we are a band of brothers forged under battle. We would all give our lives for each other, but the only member not tested was Rahim.

At 1600 hours I got a call on the hot line from Captain Sessions, "Jack, the Colonel told me to call you after we cleared the church. He said you wanted to come and search for al-Qaida funds hidden here."

"Yes, Captain, that is correct. We think there may be some kind of money hidden there. Did you guys find anything?"

"We killed eight al-Qaida and found a lot of information including phones and computer tablets. We have an organizational chart and the headman was Aamir not Abdul Aalee."

"Wow, that is a surprise!"

"Yes, a big surprise. If you want to come here I cannot offer any protection because this area is still hot. Al-Qaida could be anywhere around here. I will call you back when I think is safe for your group."

"Jack, we have the road cleared all the way here. I will tell my men at the check points to let you pass. We have cleared all the buildings between the island and here except for the college. I repeat do not come now wait until I call you back in a few hours."

"Roger that Captain, we will wait for your call. We will be driving a blue ford truck and a black ford truck."

"Okay, Jack, talk to you later. We are encountering heavy gunfire, got to go."

I could hear in the background heavy gunfire and someone yell RPG! I told everyone the church is too hot right now and Sessions will call us back when it is safe. I also told them about Aamir being the headman in the al-Qaida organization.

Eddie said, "See, you cannot trust anyone. You still want to bring Rahim with us?"

"Yes I do Eddie, Rahim is harmless. Now we wait for Sessions to call us back. I hope it is soon because in a few hours it will be dark and we are not going there at night. Everyone double check all the gear."

When Captain Sessions called us it was 1600 hours, checking my watch it was now 1800 hours, and no call back yet. It will be dark in another two hours so I think we will wait until tomorrow for the search.

It was now 2100 hours and still no phone call so I called him but no one answered. I tried again, no answer again. Now I was worried about Captain Sessions so I called Colonel Turner and received no answer. What the hell is going on? I got on the military radio given to me by Colonel Turner but no reply.

It was dark now and we could not see them but only heard the old Black Hawk helicopters flying back to the Fort. I thought maybe I should drive to the Fort and see what is going on.

All of a sudden my phone rang, "Hello, Jack here."

I put on the speaker so everyone could hear the

call.

"Jack, this is Turner, I got bad news. Captain Sessions is missing. Sessions was in a gun battle with the enemy at the church and that is the last time I spoke to him. They were out gunned, by the time we got there four of his men were killed, and he is missing. I think you were right about the church being al-Qaida HQ as they are really fighting to protect that church for some reason."

"Colonel, what can we do to help?"

"Jack double check your security and protect Camp Tocabaga. Stay alert keep on your toes these guys are tricky. We will not give up our search for Captain Sessions. Bye for now."

The phone call ended just as it started to rain again. Another thunderstorm was coming in and the wind kicked up to about 40mph making everyone chilly for a change as the temperature dropped to about 60 degrees.

It was too late and too dangerous to go search the church for al-Qaida funds. I worried about Captain Sessions but I couldn't do anything about that right now. I prayed for all the Rangers.

Should we go to the church anyway tomorrow to help find Sessions and search for the hidden funds or stay here and be safe? Being safe was not my style so if the others agree we would go tomorrow.

As I pledged it was now my mission to save as many kids as I can and bring them here to Tocabaga to live in safety. If they have no parents then someone here will take them into their family. We have good generous people living here; we help each other stay alive.

These past five days have worn me out I need some rest. I need a vacation. I need to go somewhere away from all this madness. The stress is getting to me. I wonder what ever happened to Disney World. I went there years ago when my kids were little; it was a fun time. Now there are no more fun times, just dangerous times.

I am too tried to write any more now.

That is all for now.

God Bless America,
Jack Gunn

ARTICLE: GUN SELECTION

When al-Qaida comes for you and your loved ones you better have a gun. This article will cover gun selection based on what is the most popular ammunition. The gun is your most important asset. Without ammunition however, your gun is worthless. What kind of guns should one own? Based on my 40 years of gun experience the type of gun and caliber is very important for your protection. Guns have only two main purposes which are hunting and self protection. Of course any of the guns mentioned in this article can be used for hunting as well as self defense. The question is which gun is the best tool for the job.

For people new to guns I try to explain the differences in a simple manner. When purchasing your first gun it is a confusing matter to choose the correct gun with the large selection in the market. I have had many people ask me, what type of gun should I purchase? Where do you go to learn to shoot?

GUNS FOR HUNTING

The most popular ammunition is the .22 long and the 12 gauge shot gun round. This ammo is easy to obtain and that is what is important. The more popular the ammo is the easier it is to find when you run out of ammunition. I break down guns into two categories which are hunting guns and tactical guns or combat weapons.

There may come a time when you will need to hunt for food. There are two types of hunting guns that can dispatch most animals and that is a 12 gauge shot gun and a .22 caliber rifle or pistol. These two guns allow you good flexibility. The shot gun you can use bird shot for hunting birds or rabbits and slugs for hunting deer or larger animals. In addition a 12 gauge with slugs or buck shot is a great weapon to use for protection at close range.

The one drawback is that shot gun shells are expensive and heavy to carry and too large to store many of them. Shot guns come mostly in semi automatic and pump type. They hold 5 to 8 rounds. The difference is the semi auto you just load and pull the trigger. The faster you pull the trigger the faster it shoots. The pump needs to be pumped or cocked each time to shoot it. I prefer the semi auto type because it is faster, easier to clean and use. Double barrel or single shot shotguns are not worth owning since you have to reload every time you fire it.

Do not under estimate the .22 rifle or long barrel pistol as it can be used on birds and or small rodents as well as be a tool for self defense. A .22 with hollow point bullets is an easy weapon to use and you can carry a lot of ammunition since the bullets are so small. You can store 5,000 rounds of this ammo in a desk due to its small size. A .22 rifle has a 200 yard range and 6 inch barrel pistol has a 50 yard range.

The 12 gauge shot gun and a .22caliber rifle are a must to own. A .22 rifle also comes in pump or semi auto types. The choice is up to you. As for 22 pistols there is only one that I will mention and that is the Ruger target model as it is the best you can buy.

My selection for a shotgun is a Remington semi auto model that handles 2 ¾ inch shells. Purchase a shotgun that has a stock and forearm that is made of modern plastic as it can stand up better to the elements.

GUNS FOR SELF DEFENSE

There are many types of combat pistol and rifle ammunition. The selection of the ammunition is critical to the type of combat rifle or combat pistol you will select for protection. The shotgun and .22 rifle mentioned above are dual purpose weapons but are mainly for hunting. The pistols and rifles mentioned below are really the weapons you need for total protection. These are guns that contain high capacity magazines.

What other types of guns do you need to survive? Well let us first look at what is the most popular type of ammunition used to make our selection. Having enough ammo will be your biggest problem. The fact is most police and military hand guns are 9 mm. The 45 caliber and 40 calibers are also popular but not as common as 9mm luger ammo. The 9mm ammo is also less expensive to purchase.

For rifles there are only three major types of calibers that are widely used by the police and military. One is the .223 Winchester also known as the 5.56mm NATO round. The other is the AK 47 round 7.62 x39, a round used by the military and some police around the world. This is the most popular ammo used by terrorists and gangs because the AK 47 is an inexpensive weapon or rifle. The last is the .308 Winchester round or 7.62x51 NATO.

The .223 ammo is used by the famous Colt AR15 or the M16 which is now named the M4 carbine, widely used by our military. There are many different manufactures of the so called AR15 design. Some of these AR designs also shoot 7.62x51 NATO which is the basically the same as the .308 Winchester and are called AR10 rifles.

The 7.62x39 and 7.62x51 are not to be confused as they are totally different rounds. The drawback of the 7.62x51round is the cost is higher than the .223 and when you are hauling around 300 rounds they are also heavier. The 7.62 x 51 is a long range round and can exceed 800 yards. The .223 round has an effective range of up to 500 yards.

You can also purchase an AR type rifle that will fire the AK 47 7.62x39mm round. Bushmaster is one of the best manufactures for AR type designs which can be purchased in many different calibers. Several companies also make a .22 caliber AR rifle such as Colt and the Smith and Wesson M&P 15-22.

The most popular type ammunition for a pistol is the 9mm luger round. The most common type for a rifle is the .223 Winchester also known as the 5.56mmNATO round. Knowing this we can select a number of different pistols, rifles, or carbines to use. For this selection we need to keep in mind durability, ease of cleaning, interchangeability, and ease of use by men or women.

Knowing that we want a hand gun that shoots 9mm luger rounds you can note that all 9mm are semi auto design and are not revolvers. Semi auto means it has a magazine that holds the bullets and some can hold up to 18 rounds before reloading. There are two hand guns that I recommend which are a Glock and a Springfield Armory model XD. I own both and they are the best dependable hand guns on the market. This is not to say there are not other good brands but based on my shooting experience buying one of these handguns you cannot go wrong.

My favorite however is the Glock Model 17 because it is dependable and very easy to clean and repair. Yes, sometimes guns break so you should have some extra parts or a backup gun or two if possible. Each gun comes with an assembly manual and the Glock can be taken apart by just removing the slide and one pin which is pushed out. I have shot thousands of rounds and only had my Glock break one time. The trigger return spring broke and I replaced in 10 minutes with a new one. It is so simple that anyone can work on it. The Glock can be dropped in the mud, run over by a truck and still shoot. It can be fired under water and the barrel life is 350,000 rounds which is more than you will ever shoot in your life time.

Basically all AR15 type rifles are the same design and are easy to take apart for cleaning. The models may have different names from different manufactures such as Armalite SPR Mod 1 which is basically the same as a Colt CAR15 or carbine model of the AR 15 rifle.

It pays to buy a good quality rifle from a well known manufacturer even if it may cost a little more. Remember your life may depend on this weapon. If you buy an AR type rifle then find out what parts you may need to replace by asking the manufacture. I recommend buying two weapons of the same type this way you have a back up and you do not have to learn about different weapons and the assemblies. Parts between different manufactures' are not necessarily interchangeable. The AR15 can be cleaned in about 10 minutes just by pushing out a pin which opens the rifle up. It is also light weight so men and women can use it. The recoil is very low which is important for accurate firing. I recommend the Colt brand AR15 .223 as this is a dependable weapon which has been on the market many years.

Some manufactures such as Colt have also made CAR15 carbines that use the pistol 9mm luger round. This is an excellent weapon that has very little recoil but has a limited range of about 100 yards. It is made for close quarter combat situations. Having a CAR15 9mm is a good choice since you can use the same ammo as your 9mm hand gun.

To summarize the guns needed are; a 12 gauge shotgun semi automatic type, a .22 rifle or target pistol, a 9mm luger Glock hand gun, and a .223 (5.56 NATO) AR15 design rifle or a CAR15 9mm carbine. I would choose to have two guns of each type so you have a backup. How much ammo do you need? It is up to you to decide, but the more the better as the gun is worthless without ammunition. If you can only own one or two guns then the AR15 rifle and the 9mm Glock are my choices.

Everyone in your family should know how to shoot each type of gun. I suggest one gun for each family member. Gun selection should be made by what each member of the family likes best to shoot. One may like a .22 caliber and one may like a 9mm Glock. Remember your family is also your Army to help protect each other. So proper training is very important. Do not spare any expense on training. Do not buy cheap unreliable guns.

GUN SAFETY

If you have no experience with guns then it is suggested
that you learn by going to your local gun store or
shooting range and take lessons from a good instructor.
If you have a friend who shoots go with him to the
range. The National Rifle Association or NRA is a
valuable resource to use for this learning process.

NRA has safety rules which you can find listed on line.
 The worst thing you can do is buy a gun and not know
how to use it or even load it. If you are faced with a
threat to your life or that of your family then you better
know how to use the weapon with some degree of skill.
The more skillful you are the better your chance of
survival will be. We are talking life and death situations
that require split second decisions on your part so
shooting practice is a very necessary. Join a local
shooting club.

I stress do not buy a gun just to have one. Do not buy a
gun if you will never practice or shoot it. How much
practice do you need? Based on my experience I think
shooting your weapon at least one to two hours per
week is necessary to become a good shot and learn to
know everything about your gun. I know many people
who shoot two hours a week. I also stress go take
combat shooting lessons at a gun school such as Gun

Sight or Front Sight. They will train you in Home Defense, Vehicle Defense, Tactical Rifle, Pistol, and Shotgun use. Be the best you can be as learning to shoot is more than just going to the range and pulling the trigger.

Above all be a safe shooter and follow the safety rules. When not in use keep you guns locked up so kids cannot access them and they cannot be stolen from you. I strongly suggest a gun safe to store your guns and ammo as it will give you peace of mind. You can also keep other valuables in the safe. Shooting can be a great hobby providing much enjoyment and fun for the whole family. Learning how to shoot can save your life. Shoot safe and shoot straight.